COACHES IN AND AROUND BRIGHTON

COACHES IN AND AROUND BRIGHTON

SIMON STANFORD

AMBERLEY

Front cover: Capturing a typical Brighton coaching scene on Madeira Drive, a sunny day and some of Brighton's stunning architecture in the background. Bedford Duple Dominant OBW 140P from the Campings Coaches fleet, with advert boards for excursions to a variety of destinations including Marwell Zoo, Kent Blossom tour and Winchelsea/Rye. (Nigel Lukowski)

Rear cover: Goodwood Races is the destination on offer here from Unique Coaches. YCD 880K, their immaculate Bedford YRQ with Duple Viceroy bodywork, is seen on Marine Parade in September 1976. (Stuart Little)

First published 2019

Amberley Publishing
The Hill, Stroud
Gloucestershire, GL5 4EP

www.amberley-books.com

Copyright © Simon Stanford, 2019

The right of Simon Stanford to be identified as the Author of this work has been asserted in accordance with the Copyrights, Designs and Patents Act 1988.

ISBN 978 1 4456 8541 0 (print)
ISBN 978 1 4456 8542 7 (ebook)

British Library Cataloguing in Publication Data.
A catalogue record for this book is available from the British Library.

Typesetting by Aura Technology and Software Services, India. Printed in the UK.

Introduction

Many people have said to me over the years, 'It's in the blood'. They are referring to coaches of course and they are right – I cannot stay away from them. From driving them to repairing them, photographing them and owning one, I have enjoyed them immensely. After all, I have spent all my life connected to coaching in some way, with almost a forty-year career in the bus and coach business in various roles.

This book shares my personal memories of coaching in Brighton from the early sixties to the nineties. The photographs chosen attempt to replicate this time and the types of coaches I remember only too well: Bedfords with bodies by Duple and Plaxton, Southdown Leylands, and not forgetting the Harrington coach body made in Hove, a short distance from Brighton. For me, locations such as the seafront, Marine Parade, the Old Steine, the aquarium and Pool Valley were the heart of the Brighton coaching scene, with much variety to be found in operators and coaches alike. Look out for Brighton's wonderful Regency and Georgian architecture, the magnificent buildings, lovely floral gardens and icons such as Concorde and Forte's restaurants, and the unmistakable arches along Madeira Drive, where many of these photographs were taken.

I was born in Brighton and grew up there. My father was a coach driver for Campings Coaches in Brighton for most of his working life, and from a very young age I would go with him to work at every opportunity – be this an excursion or workers' contracts. As such, I have fond memories of sitting on the engine cover of a Bedford or Thames Duple coach, having passengers pat me on the head and give me sweets as they got off the coach, or watching Dad take part in the Brighton coach rally. Equally enjoyable was spending time at the garage in Hollingdean. I will always remember my first introduction to the smell of diesel and oil! Family holidays – yes, you've guessed it – were by coach, with the West Country and Wales being popular destinations as I recall.

Brighton is famous for many things, but for me it was the coaching season, traditionally beginning around Easter. Madeira Drive, along Brighton seafront, would see a line-up of coaches from the four main operators in the town – Southdown, Campings, Unique and Alpha – plying their trade to intending excursion customers. Boards would be lined up along the sides of the coaches advertising forthcoming excursions. Full- or half-day tours were offered to destinations such as Compton Acres, Petworth, Arundel, Hastings and Chessington Zoo, before it became Chessington World of Adventures. The ever-popular Ashdown Forest tour would be on offer for local and regular passengers, as well as visitors staying in the town, not forgetting that all-important stop for tea. Sometimes Dad would take passengers during the summer season on an 'evening run', as he called it. This time it would be a pub stop on the way home. So popular was the excursion season that coaches would be seen parked on the seafront every day of the week, but Sunday was the most popular, with several full coaches departing for an afternoon excursion. Campings had an office next to the aquarium, which is visible in some of the photographs included in this book, and Southdown had one next to Palace Pier, where you could book your trips out or holidays well in advance; there were no online bookings in those days! Unique and Alpha would have advert boards outside their premises in the town. Unique's forte seemed to be race meeting excursions; I recall Goodwood races being a common one for them. One year an adventurous extended trip for Campings was for the Blackpool Illuminations. The tour began with overnight travel on a Bedford Plaxton, arriving in Blackpool early in the morning. An evening tour along Blackpool seafront to see the illuminations finished off the day, and then home.

April was an important month in the coach operator's diary, and mine too, as it was the month in which the British Coach Rally was held, with it taking place on Madeira Drive each year from 1956. This provided operators from around the UK, as well as some foreign entrants, the opportunity to show off their new coach deliveries for the forthcoming season, and an impressive line-up of coaches from a variety of manufacturers, all gleaming in the Brighton sunshine, would adorn Madeira Drive.

Day trippers to Brighton in the summer would be dropped off along the seafront and drivers would park up for the day at the eastern end of the seafront at Dukes Mound. When parking there was full, they would head towards Roedean, further east, to find additional parking. Some busy weekends would see Brighton station car park take the overflow of visiting coaches. Operators such as Venture, Golden Miller, Grey Green, Lacey's and Lewis would each see two or three coaches arriving in Brighton.

I have selected specific photographs to recall an era of coaching in Brighton as I remember and enjoyed it from the sixties to the nineties. Photographs were taken in locations around Brighton and Hove, with Madeira Drive being the most popular location for local excursion coaches to ply their trade and visiting coaches to drop off their passengers and the coach rally held here for many years. The Old Steine and Brighton's coach station, Pool Valley, are recalled too. Photographs featured come from a vast collection I have taken and collected over many years, as well as many obtained from renowned bus and coach photographers only too pleased to help me put together this publication.

I hope you enjoy this journey back in time as much as I have.

Simon Stanford

This Campings Duple-bodied Ford Thames could carry forty-one passengers. New in 1961, it was entered in that year's Brighton Coach Rally. This photo was taken not far from my family home in Hove – no doubt Dad was home for lunch. (D. Warren)

On a damp Madeira Drive, and attracting few passengers it seems, is a Campings Bedford Duple. This forty-one-seat Super Vega was new in 1961. (PM Photography)

Departing from Madeira Drive with a full compliment of passengers for an afternoon excursion, this Campings Bedford Duple is driven on this occasion by my father, Steve. (R. H. G. Simpson)

A rather wet and deserted Madeira Drive sees a Campings Bedford Duple in company with a Southdown Weymann-bodied Leyland Leopard. (PM Photography)

Campings on tour. Duple Bella Vega-bodied Bedford SB5, new to Whittle coaches in 1963, is seen in Torquay in 1964. I recall spending many holidays aboard a Campings coach as a child. Who knows, I may have been on this one! (J. S. Cockshot)

Parked west along the seafront from Madeira Drive is WNG 662, a 1957 Bedford Duple seen carrying a variation from the traditional red and blue Campings livery. Alfriston is the destination for today's excursion. (PM Photography)

Campings operated several twin-steer Bedford VAL coaches. This fifty-two-seat Duple Vega, new in 1966, was painted in the traditional red and blue livery with a white roof. (SEC)C. Warren

Entry 1 in the 1978 Brighton Coach Rally was a Campings Bedford Plaxton Supreme. Having received a new body, it looks rather splendid in their revised livery. (PM Photography)

Entry 53 in the 1976 Brighton Coach Rally was a Campings Seddon with Duple Viceroy bodywork. (PM Photography)

Seen basking in the sun at the 1975 Brighton Coach Rally is this fifty-one-seat, Duple-bodied Seddon, new in 1972. Campings operated at least three Seddons – a change from the Bedfords or Fords normally operated. (Edward Busst)

New to Best Tours in London is Campings Bristol LH JAR 629G, which received a new Plaxton body in 1970 when only a year old. (PM Photography)

Another Seddon in the Campings fleet with Duple's Viceroy bodywork, ERM 117K is seen on Marine Parade, about to depart for an afternoon excursion. Marine Parade was used for local excursion coaches when Madeira Drive was closed for events. (PM Photography)

A rare coach for a Brighton operator is this Caetano Cascais-bodied Bedford, which looks very smart indeed and suits this style of Campings' livery. The more traditional Bedford Duple operating with Unique Coaches can be seen behind. (PM Photography)

A typical busy summer afternoon in Brighton. Passing the aquarium and the Campings kiosk on an afternoon excursion is EAD 960C, a Bedford SB5 with a Duple forty-one-seat body. (PM Photography)

Coventry is the location for this pair of Campings coaches in October 1967. On the left EAD960C is a Bedford and right is FPM871C, a Ford, both bodied by Duple. (Robert F. Mack)

At the aquarium roundabout, Campings CTM 406D – a Ford with fifty-two-seat Duple bodywork – and a coach operated by Unique Coaches are seen leaving Madeira Drive for an afternoon excursion. (PM Photography)

Seen on Brighton's marine parade is a trio of Duple Dominants. Campings, Unique and Alpha all operated forty-five-seat Bedfords for excursion customers. Who remembers green shield stamps? The garage opposite is a reminder of those days when these were given out with fuel purchases. (PM Photography)

Formally Campings LBU 153L, DBY 310 looks very different from her former life in Brighton, having undergone many modifications. Photographed in Valetta, Malta, in 2010, she was still giving sterling service despite her thirty-seven years. Several Bedfords with Duple and Plaxton bodywork from Sussex saw further service in Malta.

Another Campings Bedford VAL twin steer with Duple Viceroy fifty-three-seat bodywork, PTO 667G was new to a Nottingham-based company in 1968. (PM Photography)

This forty-one-seat Bedford Plaxton was new in 1970. When her passenger-carrying days were over she became a traveller's home but was sadly scrapped in 1995. (PM Photography)

The rain hasn't deterred passengers boarding excursion coaches on Madeira Drive today. Bound for Ashdown Forest is Campings LRO 143L, a Bedford with Duple Dominant forty-five-seat bodywork. (PM Photography)

Campings Ford Duple Dominant PFR 266M was new to a Blackpool-based operator. It is seen here leaving Madeira Drive on an excursion, with another Campings behind. (Robert F. Mack)

This Plaxton-bodied LH started life in the North East of England. Campings operated it in Brighton, before it ended its days in southern Ireland. It was photographed on Marine Parade with a variety of excursions on offer. (PM Photography)

New to the Kings Ferry coach company in 1976, NBH 111P was a Brighton Coach Rally entrant in April of that year. Note the unusual flat side windows fitted to this Duple Dominant-bodied Bedford. (PM Photography)

A colour shot of NBH 111P in 1982, showing the traditional red, blue and white of Campings as I fondly remembered it. (Nigel Lukowski)

The passengers are all aboard for an afternoon excursion from Madeira Drive. Campings OBW 139P is sister to OBW 140P – the coach on the front cover. While OBW 139P featured slightly more white in the livery, OBW 140P retained more of its previous owner's livery (Carterton Coaches). (Nigel Lukowski)

A sunny day on Madeira Drive sees Plaxton Supreme-bodied Bedford YNT WFX 73X, which was new in 1982. This photo was taken just after Campings were taken over by Brighton Borough Transport in 1989. (The Omnibus Society)

Campings Bedford Plaxton Supreme WFX 73X was new to Marchwood Motorways of Southampton. It is seen here on Madeira Drive, continuing the excursion tradition. (Nigel Lukowski)

A colourful and floral Old Steine, Brighton. Campings WFX 73X is seen soon after the takeover by Brighton Borough Transport; their legal address is visible just forward of the rear wheels.

Campings forty-five-seat Bedford Plaxton RPE 450R was new to Bexleyheath Transport in Kent, a frequent visitor to Brighton. This photo was taken on Madeira Drive in 1983. Note the excursion boards in the side windows. (Nigel Lukowski)

A February 1980 view of Brighton. Where the old Kemp Town railway station forecourt would have been is Campings Bedford Plaxton Elite LRO 142L. (Nigel Lukowski)

Rebodied Bedford Plaxton RUF 621R. New in 1977, it is seen sporting a much revised livery on Madeira Drive in 1982. Behind are coaches of Alpha and Southdown – all on excursion duties. (Nigel Lukowski)

A very smart Bedford Duple Dominant with more white in the livery than usual. Campings excursions on offer included trips to Hampton Court and the ever-popular Ashdown Forest tour, including a stop for afternoon tea. (Nigel Lukowski)

The Bedford chassis bodied by Plaxton or Duple was the mainstay of Brighton coach operators for many years. This Duple example was photographed in the Old Steine in 1989, soon after the Brighton Borough Transport takeover. (Nigel Lukowski)

New in 1980 to a Welsh operator, this Bedford Duple was photographed leaving Madeira Drive with a full complement of passengers in 1982. It is looking very smart indeed in this revised livery. (Nigel Lukowski)

CAX 15V is seen on Madeira Drive in 1989 under Brighton Borough Transport ownership. Note the return to the more traditional livery. (Nigel Lukowski)

Working a courtesy coach service in 1989 from the Brighton centre to the Metropole Hotel, Campings Bedford Plaxton REA 946W is seen while in Brighton Borough Transport ownership. (Nigel Lukowski)

PJT 523W was new to Excelsior Coaches, Bournemouth, in 1981. It is seen taking part in the 1983 Coach Rally on Madeira Drive. (Nigel Lukowski)

Campings Ford Plaxton PJT 523W on a deserted Madeira Drive. Excursion boards are displayed in the side windows. (Nigel Lukowski)

PJT 523W is seen again, this time on a busy Brighton seafront while working a courtesy coach service to the Metropole Hotel. (Nigel Lukowski)

Campings Bedford Plaxton GBO 241W was new to Hills Coaches, Tredegar, South Wales, in 1980. When her service in Brighton was over she returned home to Wales to another Welsh operator. She is seen here at the Brighton Centre. (Nigel Lukowski)

PTX 331Y, seen on Marine Parade, is a Bedford YNT with Plaxton Supreme V1 coachwork. Note the shallow and flat side glazing. A variety of excursions are on offer today. (PM Photography)

An offside colour view of PTX 331Y, again seen on Madeira Drive. (Nigel Lukowski)

Campings were regular participants at the Brighton Coach Rally. Bedford Plaxton Supreme EUR 525Y was Entrant 3 in the 1985 event, which took place as usual on Madeira Drive.

EUR 525Y returns to Sussex. It escaped with only minor damage in the Campings depot fire in 1987. It is seen here in Eastbourne, looking very smartly turned out with Hancocks Coaches.

Seating just thirty-five passengers, Campings Ford Plaxton NMC 66X is seen at their Portslade depot. This coach formed part of the fleet taken over by Brighton Borough Transport in 1989 and was repainted in that operator's corporate blue and white livery. (Nigel Lukowski)

A wintry scene in Portland Road, Hove, for A840 PPP in January 1991. This Bedford is in Brighton Borough Transport coach livery with Campings fleet names. (Nigel Lukowski)

TSV 717 was new as B272 HCD with BCP Parking in Crawley. It later received Brighton Borough Transport blue and white coach livery and Lewes Coaches fleet names. (Nigel Lukowski)

VCD 10, a baby Bedford Duple new to Alpha Coaches in 1958, is seen in Madeira Drive. (PM Photography)

VJD 469, a 1962 Bedford with Plaxton Embassy bodywork, is seen on Brighton's Madeira Drive in August 1969 while under the ownership of Alpha Coaches. (Mike Street)

A wonderful view of Alpha Coaches' premises in Brighton. Seen parked outside is Bedford Duple Vega UUF 460, a forty-one seater that was new in 1957. (PM Photography)

Alpha Coaches 1965 Ford CCD 370C had Harrington Legionnaire bodywork. The Harrington factory was a short distance away in Hove and sadly closed in around 1966. This splendid rear view of CCD 370C is seen on Madeira Drive. (PM Photography)

Alpha Coaches Bedford Duples CUF 553L and CUF 554L were new in 1973. CUF 553 is seen loading passengers for an afternoon excursion on Marine Parade. (PM Photography)

A wet Brighton seafront in May 1973 sees Alpha Coaches CUF 554L trying to attract excursion customers. (C. Warren)

An array of excursions on offer from Alpha's Bedford Duple JVJ 442P in this 1976 view. This coach, one of at least seven coaches to have operated in Sussex, was exported to Malta and became DBY 447. (PM Photography)

A slightly different view of Alpha Coaches Duple Dominant JVJ 442P, with a Campings Bedford Plaxton behind. (Edward Busst)

Mayfield and Rotherfield and a mystery drive are excursions on offer with Alpha Coaches today. This Bedford Duple Dominant was new to Whittle Coaches. A Bedford Duple Viceroy operated by Unique Coaches can be seen behind. (PM Photography)

Another view of Alpha Coaches Bedford Duple Dominant LUX 501P. Note the usual high standard of presentation. (PM Photography)

Displaying excursion boards inside the coach, Alpha Coaches EAP 911V is seen between two Campings coaches on Madeira Drive. (PM Photography)

Rear views are vital when recording the photographic history of buses and coaches. This view of Alpha Coaches Bedford Plaxton EAP 911V highlights the use of the boot lid to record the company name, address and phone number. Nowadays we would see a web and email address. (Robert F. Mack)

Alpha entered two new Bedfords in the 1980 Brighton Coach Rally. On the left is a twenty-nine-seat Duple-bodied VAS5, while on the right is a Duple-bodied YLQ seating forty-five. (PM Photography)

Alpha exhibited their new 1983 Leyland Tiger with Plaxton Paramount bodywork in that year's Brighton Coach Rally. With Alpha Holidays fleet names, the coach featured holiday destinations such as Llandudno and the Lake District in the side windows. This view shows the Tiger approaching the aquarium roundabout. (PM Photography)

Alpha Coaches D83 WWV, a Bedford YNV with Duple coachwork, is seen on Marine Parade. A Campings Plaxton Supreme also on excursion duties sits behind. (PM Photography)

The races were a popular event for excursion and private hire customers from Brighton. Alpha Coaches Bedford Duple D921 GRU is seen at the Epsom Derby in 1988. (PM Photography)

Alpha Volvo KBZ 2476. The Plaxton Paramount bodywork shows this livery to great effect. Cherished registrations, or private plates as they are sometimes referred to, became popular among coach operators in the 1980s. (PM Photography)

Another Alpha Coaches Plaxton Paramount dating from 1984; this one is a Bedford YMP seating thirty-five. The Alpha Holidays name became standard in the late 1980s. (PM Photography)

Bedford SB3 XOD 403 was new to a Torquay, Devon, operator, but is seen in Brighton while operating in British Radio Corporation livery. The red and blue livery is not dissimilar to Campings'. It was not uncommon for firms to operate their own coaches to transport staff, or indeed to hire in coaches on a contract basis.

A little older than I remember but I could not resist including KUF 51. This splendid Leyland Comet with a thirty-two-seat, locally built Harrington body dated from 1950. Sadly, this black and white photo does not show the green Unique Coaches livery to great effect. In this view she is parked on Brighton seafront opposite the Pool Valley exit. (PM Photography)

Another oldie, and again before my time, but Bedford OBs are stunning little coaches. Information on this Unique Coaches example is sparse, but again I could not resist including her. (PM Photography)

It is remarkable how this Bedford Duple, which was new in 1958 to Unique Coaches, was twelve years old when this photo was taken on Madeira Drive in 1970. It is a credit to that operator. (John Stringer)

A colourful Madeira Drive with Unique and Campings coaches touting for excursion customers. Bedford Duple UUF 600 was new in 1958 with a lovely two-tone green livery. (PM Photography)

Note the police notice stating that there is no parking here! I am sure this doesn't apply to 1800 CD, a Harrington-bodied Bedford from Unique Coaches, seen on Marine Parade. (PM Photography)

Unique Coaches Harrington-bodied Bedford 5858 CD and a Campings Bedford Duple on a quiet Madeira Drive. (PM Photography)

An afternoon excursion hosted by Unique Coaches departing for Sheffield Park Gardens at 2.30 p.m. (PM Photography)

It is 1972 on Brighton's Madeira Drive and Unique Coaches Harrington-bodied Bedford CUF 600C is looking as splendid as always. (John Kaye)

Unique Coaches Bedford CUF 600C, with Harrington Crusader coachwork, was seen in 1969. Note the open-top Brighton Hove & District Bristol passing by on the 17 service. (Mike Street)

Life after Unique Coaches. Harrington-bodied Bedford CUF 600C still shows a Brighton destination when photographed in Hove. (Nigel Lukowski)

Unique Coaches Bedford NCD 122M, with Duple Dominant bodywork, is seen on excursion duties. The two-tone green livery is shown here to great effect. (Edward Busst)

Unique Coaches Bedford Duple Dominant PUF 794M is seen on Madeira Drive in 1975. (Edward Busst)

Unique Coaches Duple Dominant PUF 794M is photographed approaching the Old Steine, about to take up excursion duties on the seafront. The forty-five-seat Bedford was the mainstay of small independent operators of this period. (PM Photography)

With driver's deck chair in place, Unique Coaches Bedford Duple MRV 631R is hoping to attract passengers for Bodiam and Hastings. The fare is £1.70 per passenger. (PM Photography)

Seen along the seafront in Hove is a Unique Coaches Bedford Duple Dominant. Looking rather bland and without any fleet names, the livery is a far cry from the Unique from the 1960s and 1970s with their two-tone green. (Nigel Lukowski)

A rear view of Unique Coaches Duple Dominant-bodied Bedford CNJ 945T, with Campings NBH 111P in front. Madeira Drive is the location, with the Palace Pier just visible. (PM Photography)

AYJ 987T, a Bedford with Duple Dominant bodywork, is photographed along Madeira Drive. (Nigel Lukowski)

A rear view of Unique Coaches Bedford Duple AYJ 987T in North Street, Brighton. Note the rhombus shape used for the Unique fleet name. (Robert F. Mack)

Southdown Motor Services 60 AUF, a 1962 Commer Avenger with Harrington Crusader coachwork, is photographed in Pool Valley in 1969. After Southdown, 60 AUF gained the registration WTS 429A and became a traveller's home. (Mike Street)

Celebrating 100 years of Southdown in 2015, a special event took place in Southsea. The beautifully restored Harrington Cavalier-bodied Leyland Leopard 749 DCD is seen here representing a golden age of coaching. Southdown were a loyal operator of Harrington-bodied coaches.

A marvellous 1964 view of a Southdown Leyland Leopard with Plaxton Panorama bodywork leaving Brighton for an excursion in company with a Unique Harrington coach. Note the Southdown driver in full uniform. (SEC)

Southdown 8733 CD, a Leyland Leopard with Harrington Cavalier bodywork, was new in 1961 and fitted with twenty-eight seats for tours. Now seating forty-one, it is seen on Madeira Drive advertising an afternoon mid-Sussex tour. (S. J. Butler)

Another Southdown coach restored and in attendance at the Southdown 100 event in Southsea, this 1960 Leyland Tiger Cub is fitted with Weymann Fanfare coachwork.

Becoming part of the National Bus Company brought with it a bland white livery, replacing the traditional two-tone Southdown green. Southdown BUF 84C is seen on Madeira Drive ready to take up excursion duties. (Harry Hay/Bus Archive)

It is 1966 and Wannock Gardens is the afternoon excursion destination for EUF 192D, a Leyland Leopard with a Plaxton Panorama body. Behind is a Campings Duple Vega, also on excursion duty. (SEC)

Many Southdown buses and coaches found new owners after disposal. This was probably due to their high standards of maintenance. Formerly 1785, HCD 385E – a Leyland Leopard with Duple bodywork – stayed local, finding a new owner in Hove. (Nigel Lukowski)

London-bound in 1980, Southdown Leyland Plaxton LCD 228F is seen in Pool Valley. Wearing National white livery, it is looking good despite its twelve years. (Nigel Lukowski)

This former Southdown Leyland Leopard returned to Sussex in August 1987. It was in use with Kidlington Band from Oxford when it posed for Nigel Lukowski's camera by the Palace Pier. Note the Maidstone & District Invictaway double-decker paying Brighton a visit.

LCD 247F, a Southdown Leyland Leopard Plaxton Panorama with forty-nine-seat coachwork, is photographed on Madeira Drive in 1969. A Campings Bedford Duple is behind. (Mike Street)

My favourite Southdown vehicle type was definitely the Leyland Leopard with Northern Counties dual-purpose bodywork. Although primarily used on bus work, PUF 165H is working 064 express service to London when seen in 1978. From a batch of thirty new to Southdown, two survive in preservation, including this one. (SEC)

Taking part in the 1970 Coach Rally on Madeira Drive was Southdown RUF 803H, a Duple Commander-bodied Leyland Leopard that was new that year and is seen in the traditional Southdown livery. When new these coaches would seat only thirty-two passengers; imagine the ample legroom. (SEC)

Former Southdown Leyland Leopard Plaxton Elite UUF 321J, now in the Maidstone & District fleet, boards passengers for Gillingham in this busy Pool Valley scene from July 1980. (Nigel Lukowski)

Posing in the sun and looking rather splendid following the return to traditional livery is Southdown UUF 322J. It is seen in company with an Alpha coach on excursion duties in 1981. (Barry Francis)

Another 1981 view and Southdown UUF 323J is ten years old. It is a fine example of this operator's very high standard of presentation. (Barry Francis)

Another Southdown Plaxton Elite to return to traditional livery was UUF 331J. It is seen leaving Madeira Drive on an excursion in 1983. (Andy Gibbs)

Brighton-bound on a National Express working with a full complement of passengers is Southdown UUF 340J. This coach hailed from a batch of twenty-two Plaxton Panorama Elite-bodied Leyland Leopards that were new in 1971.

UUF 329J, a 1971 Leyland Leopard with Plaxton Elite bodywork. This coach was beautifully converted by Southdown to executive status, featuring twenty-one seats, a toilet, servery and tinted windows, to name but a few of the modifications carried out. It is seen here taking part in the 1983 Brighton Coach Rally on Madeira Drive. (Nigel Lukowski)

The stunning Brighton Belle. Formerly Southdown UUF 329J, after conversion to executive status she became the Southdown Diplomat. She later took on a new identity as the Brighton Belle, being re-registered with the former Queen Mary registration number 408 DCD and in the ownership of Brighton & Hove. She is seen here taking part in the 1986 Coach Rally on Madeira Drive.

Painted umber brown and cream to resemble the Brighton Belle Pullman train operating on the London to Brighton railway, this coach looks magnificent when seen in 1986. The attention to detail was second to none. She still survives today, having been reunited with her original registration and in the fleet of Seaford & District. (Nigel Lukowski)

Madeira Drive in May 1974, about a month into the excursion season. Southdown CUF 252L, a Leyland Leopard with a Duple Dominant body, is barely a year old in this view. (SEC)

Madeira Drive in 1986 and the Southdown divisional split saw some coaches repainted in dual-purpose livery for bus work. Note the route numbers in the windscreen. CUF 260L is allocated to the West Sussex area. (Nigel Lukowski)

Southdown's 1974 coach delivery saw thirty-seven Fords with Duple Dominant forty-nine-seat bodies enter the predominantly Leyland fleet. (Nigel Lukowski)

Hants & Dorset purchased several vehicles from Southdown, including SCD 30N, a Ford Duple. It is seen here making a return visit to Brighton in 1980. Clearly visible in this view is the Campings aquarium office, with excursion boards on display. (Nigel Lukowski)

Southdown Ford Duple SCD 33N is seen with passengers aboard for an afternoon excursion from Madeira Drive. (SEC)

A Pool Valley view of Ford Duple SCD 35N, seen working express service 064 to London. (Phil Sposito)

A 1976 view of Madeira Drive with two Southdown Plaxton Supremes awaiting excursion passengers. LWV 268P has alternate blue and red seating to match the National Bus fleet livery. (Barry Francis)

Another former Southdown coach, seen returning to Brighton, is LWV 268P, a Leyland Leopard Plaxton Supreme seen here on Madeira Drive in 1986. It is still carrying a Brighton allocation disc in the licence holder – a reminder of its Southdown days. (Nigel Lukowski)

Southdown Leyland Leopard Plaxton Supreme LWV 268P is seen leaving Pool Valley. It was one of a batch of five from the 1976 batch of coaches to wear Townsend Thoresen livery. (Andy Gibbs)

LWV 271P looks very smart in National Holidays livery. This Plaxton-bodied Leyland Leopard is on route 025 to Bournemouth when seen in Pool Valley in June 1984. (Nigel Lukowski)

Formerly LWV 272P and now carrying a Leyland PD3 Queen Mary registration number and a revised coach livery, this 1986 view of 2880 CD was taken in Pool Valley. (Nigel Lukowski)

A busy July day on Brighton's seafront in 1982 sees dual-purpose Leyland Duple RYJ 882R working the 025 express service to Portsmouth. (Nigel Lukowski)

The rail strike in 1982 brought many more passengers on to express coach services. Southdown supplied as many duplicate vehicles as possible, including double-deck buses for Brighton, Gatwick and London services. A crowd gathers to board coaches in Pool Valley for Gatwick and London. RYJ 889R is carrying Sealine 773, Brighton to Gatwick, livery. (Nigel Lukowski)

Leyland Leopard Duple RYJ 889R is photographed in a wintry February 1986, a month after the formation of Brighton & Hove, while working the limited stop Brighton–Gatwick–Guildford service. This shot was taken in the Old Steine. (Nigel Lukowski)

A Pool Valley view of Southdown's South Coast Express-liveried, Duple Dominant-bodied Leyland Leopard VCD 291S, seen working the 064 express service to London.

Brighton Marina in 1978 sees 12-metre Leyland Leopard Plaxton Supreme YYJ 300T in the short-lived Seajet livery. It was one of three coaches to wear this very attractive colour scheme. (Barry Francis)

Southdown ANJ 306T, a Leyland Leopard with Plaxton Supreme bodywork, is seen in Pool Valley in November 1985. This coach passed to Brighton & Hove soon after this photo was taken. (Nigel Lukowski)

Photographed on Brighton seafront in 1980, Southdown Leyland Leopard Duple Dominant EAP 936V is wearing the very attractive but short-lived Seajet livery. (Andy Gibbs)

EAP 936V, formerly Southdown 1336 but now Brighton & Hove 336 and newly painted in their livery, is seen photographed near to the Conway Street depot in Hove in 1986. This Leyland Leopard found fame when BT Models produced a model of it in white National livery with Brighton & Hove fleet names. (Nigel Lukowski)

A 1986 view of Pool Valley sees Brighton & Hove Leyland Leopard Duple Dominant EAP 937V and National Welsh Leyland Tiger AAL 587A. (Nigel Lukowski)

Seen in a rather deserted Pool Valley while wearing the red and cream Brighton & Hove livery is MAP 351W, a Leyland Leopard with Plaxton Supreme bodywork. (Les Simpson)

A pair of Southdown Plaxton Supremes in Pool Valley in 1981. On the left, GWV 925V (fleet number 1325) is London bound, while LPN 357W (fleet number 1357) is on a longer journey to Exeter. (Barry Francis)

TFG 221X was among the last of the Leyland Leopards delivered to Southdown in 1982. It took part in the 1983 Coach Rally on Madeira Drive along with a 1983 Leyland Tiger with Plaxton Paramount bodywork. (Alan Conway)

Seen in Brighton & Hove ownership, Duple Laser-bodied Leyland Tiger A810 CCD was one of six new to the Southdown fleet in 1984. Seen here in Pool Valley while wearing National Holidays livery, she would later wear National Express livery and was sold in 1991. (Nigel Lukowski)

New to Southdown in 1982, HHC 366Y, a Leyland Leopard with Plaxton Supreme bodywork, is seen working a 064 National Express service to London.

Another former Southdown coach to pay a return visit to Brighton seafront is A811 CCD, a 1984 Leyland Tiger bodied by Duple. New in National Holidays livery, she was transferred to Brighton & Hove in 1986 before being sold to Costin Travel in 1991. I never thought then that I was going to own it one day.

I purchased this Leyland Tiger in November 2005 and owned her for eight years. She is seen proudly on display at the Brighton & Hove 75th anniversary event on Madeira Drive in 2010, having been restored to original National Holidays livery. (Duncan Haworth)

Leaving the event and heading home after a very pleasurable day, I am captured approaching the aquarium roundabout in A811 CCD. (Duncan Haworth)

Duple Caribbean-bodied Leyland Tiger B813 JPN is seen here working a 773 service. This coach was sold in 1991 to a North Wales operator. (Nigel Lukowski)

May 1987 and Brighton & Hove B814 JPN, a Leyland Tiger with Duple Caribbean coachwork, is seen operating an express service to London. This coach was also sold in 1991 to a North Wales operator. (Nigel Lukowski)

Gales of Haslemere HPB 666N, a Duple-bodied Volvo, is seen at the Coach Rally in 1975. (Edward Busst)

Kenzie's Coaches were a regular competitor at the Coach Rally in Brighton for many years. In this 1975 view they have entered a Leyland Leopard with Duple Dominant bodywork. (Edward Busst)

An operator I always admired was Wallace Arnold, but their distinctive livery is sadly no longer around. This Duple Dominant-bodied Leyland Leopard is seen taking part in the 1975 Coach Rally in Brighton. (Edward Busst)

A coach with a pedigree; I mean AEC of course. This Reliance with Plaxton Supreme coachwork is seen on Madeira Drive in the fleet of Lewis Coaches of Greenwich. Coaches of this operator are often seen on day excursions in Brighton. (Martin Hearson)

New to Barton Transport, MRR 811K is a Plaxton-bodied AEC Reliance that seated an incredible sixty-four passengers! This was reduced to sixty when bought by London Country and it is seen here in Brighton's Pool Valley. (Les Simpson)

A rare coach spotted in Brighton's Pool Valley is GHP 994L AEC with Portuguese UTIC bodywork on a Reliance chassis, working a National Express service to Gatwick Airport. The operator is Arbutus Travel. (Paul Webber)

Parked up at the Dukes Mound end of Madeira Drive at the coach parking area is B278 KPF, a London Country Green Line Leyland Tiger with a Plaxton Paramount body. (Les Simpson)

New to Nottingham City Transport was JCH 396N, a Duple Dominant-bodied Leyland Leopard. It is seen here in use by Brighton Borough Transport at the Old Steine. (John Law)

UTD 204T, a former Southend Transport Duple-bodied Leyland Leopard, was new in 1978. The operator is Brighton Borough Transport, but it carries Lewes Coaches fleet names. This coach has an interesting history: it was rebodied in 1991 with a Willowbrook Warrior body and re-registered to PIB 5145. (John Piggott)

A visitor to Brighton's Pool Valley is East Kent MCW Metroliner B850 TKL.

C82 PRP, a Plaxton Paramount-bodied Leyland Tiger operated by United Counties, is working the National Express 325 service when seen in Pool Valley.

Southend Transport A250 SVW is seen in Pool Valley while working their 795 coach service. This coach is a Leyland Tiger with Duple Caribbean bodywork and it remains active today, having been preserved in Essex.

A 1987 Brighton Coach Rally entrant is Staffordshire-based Bassetts Coaches Leyland Tiger Plaxton Supreme XGS 764X, which is approaching the aquarium roundabout. Visible to the left of the coach is the Campings Coaches aquarium office with excursion boards on display. (PM Photography)

The Old Steine is the setting for this East Kent AEC Reliance. The chassis dates from 1973 and it was originally fitted with a Duple Dominant body. The chassis was refurbished and the new Dutch Berkhof Esprite body was fitted in 1984.

Seen outside the cinema in King's Road is Bova Futura A665 EMY from the National London fleet. Approaching behind is an Alder Valley Leyland Leopard.

A well-travelled Volvo with Duple Dominant bodywork, LPB 118P was entered in the 1980 British Coach Rally. New to Hodge Coaches of Sandhurst, and also operated with Devon-based Trathens, it is seen here with Burgess Hill Coaches, an operator based just a few miles north of Brighton. (PM Photography)

All the way from West Yorkshire, and seen working the National Express 325 service back to Bradford, is Leyland Tiger Plaxton Paramount A908 LWU.

Not all excursion passengers travel to Brighton for their day out by coach. Double-deck buses, some coach-seated, would bring day trippers to Brighton, particularly from the London area. London & Country F608 RPG, an East Lancs-bodied Dennis Dominator, is seen picking up passengers for the return journey home. Service 962 is a seaside special from West Moseley, Surrey.

Coastal Coaches was a local operator, with their base being located east of Brighton in the Newhaven/Seaford area. Entered in the 1974 Coach Rally, VMA 8J is an immaculate-looking Seddon with Plaxton Elite bodywork. Just visible behind the coach is the aquarium and the Campings booking office. (PM Photography)

Lacey's Coaches from East London were frequent visitors to Brighton, bringing day trippers to the seaside or attending the coach rally held here each year. Known for their heavyweight coaches, this Volvo, bodied by Plaxton, was entered in the 1976 Coach Rally. Note the iconic and historic arches behind the coaches along Madeira Drive. (PM Photography)

Lacey's Coaches again, this time at the 1986 Coach Rally. Proudly displaying the Tiger badge on the front grille, there is no mistaking it is a Leyland with a Duple 340 body. (PM Photography)

A pair of London Transport MCW Metrobuses seen on Brighton's Madeira Drive on a day excursion, or seaside specials as they were often referred to. (Les Simpson)

Entered in the 1967 British Coach Rally is Golden Miller Ford KPN 662E, which was bodied by Plaxton. Note the driver's bow tie and the AEC service van to the left of the coach. (PM Photography)

Golden Miller FTV 11L is a Volvo B58 with Duple Dominant bodywork. This coach was new to Skills Coaches of Nottingham and was to operate in Devon for Brixham Travel. This rear view was taken on Madeira Drive. (PM Photography)

Entrant 68 in the 1975 British Coach Rally was Golden Miller RHX 190L, a Volvo B58 with Duple Dominant coachwork. The sign in the windscreen refers to Ray Ellington, the London-born singer, drummer and band leader. It seems likely that this was the band's tour coach. (PM Photography)

New to Warrens Coaches of Ticehurst as GDY 549N, this Old Steine view of Bedford Duple OLM 873 sees it while in the fleet of Travelfar Coaches. This coach ended up as a traveller's home in the Newhaven area.

Bexleyheath Transport coaches would regularly be seen bringing day trippers to Brighton or attending the coach rally. This new Bedford Plaxton is seen in April 1977 at the 23rd British Coach Rally. Campings purchased this coach and Brighton became its home. (PM Photography)

Bexleyheath Transport YPB 842T, a Bedford Duple Dominant, is seen parked up on Madeira Drive. I always remember seeing coaches in Brighton from this firm. Their immaculate presentation was always notable. (PM Photography)

Another new Bedford for Bexleyheath Transport entered in the 1980 Coach Rally was JGU 939V. Seen in front of the arches on Madeira Drive, this coach was bodied by Duple. (PM Photography)

Bedford continued to dominate the fleet of Bexleyheath Transport with some alterations to their fleet livery. B225 OJU, a YNV with Duple Laser fifty-seven-seat bodywork, was entered in the 1985 Coach Rally. It was photographed along the eastern end of Madeira Drive. (PM Photography)

The 1986 Coach Rally entry for Bexleyheath Transport was C345 VNR, their Bedford YNV with Duple 320 bodywork, which made good use of the wide waist panels to carry enlarged fleet names. Sadly just two years later Bexleyheath would cease to trade. (PM Photography)

Acknowledgements

Many people have helped me to identify original photographers and have given permission for their use in this book. Others have donated photographs for me to use from their personal collections.

My sincere thanks go to Nigel Lukowski for his wonderful colour photographs; the late Robert F. Mack, a prolific and truly respected photographer; the Southdown Enthusiasts Club; and Phil at PM Photography for his superb collection of black and white photos. Thanks are also due to Mike Street, Duncan Haworth, John Stringer, Stuart Little, Edward Busst, Simon Butler, Barry Francis, Andy Gibbs, Alan Conway, John Law, John Kaye, Les Simpson, John Piggott, Martin Hearson, C. Warren, D. Warren, R. H. G. Simpson, Roy Marshall, Phil Sposito, Paul Webber, J. S. Cockshot, Harry Hay, and the Omnibus Society.

Thanks to you all, and my apologies if I have left anyone out.

Printed and bound by CPI Group (UK) Ltd, Croydon, CR0 4YY

30/10/2025

01988108-0006